$100M Leads

THE WORKBOOK

Disclaimer:

This workbook is intended to complement the concepts discussed in "100m Leads" by Alex Hormozi. It provides educational content, but it's not a substitute for professional advice. The author's experiences and opinions shape the content, and individual outcomes may differ. Your use of this workbook is at your own risk, and the author and publishers are not liable for any negative results. The content is protected by copyright, and unauthorized commercial use is prohibited.

SECTIONS IN THIS WORKBOOK:

1. Section 1: Start Here
- How I got Here
- The Problem This Book Solves

2. Section 2: Get Understanding
- Leads Are Not Enough
- Engage Your Leads

3. Section 3: Get Leads
- Warm Outreach
- Post Free Content Part 1
- Post Free Content Part 2
- Cold Outreach
- Run Paid Ads Part 1
- Run Paid Ads Part 2
- Core Four On Steroids

4. Section 4: Get Lead Getters
- Customer Referrals
- Employees
- Agencies
- Affiliates and Partners

5. Section 5: Get Started
- Advertising in Real Life
- The Roadmap
- A Decade in a Page

Chapter 1: Start Here

In the opening section of Chapter 1 in "100M Leads" by Alex Hormozi, the author introduces the foundational principles of money-making and highlights the crucial components involved in building a successful business. The key takeaways from this section emphasize the significance of leads, facing challenges, leveraging existing resources, quick decision-making, maximizing profit potential, and the central focus on lead generation.

The author begins by asserting that the process of making money is essentially the process of selling products or services. He stresses the necessity of understanding the complete equation—having a compelling offer, acquiring potential customers (leads), and effectively converting those leads into actual sales. This fundamental realization sets the stage for the rest of the book.

The concept of leads is explored as the linchpin for business success. Leads represent individuals who not only possess a problem that your offer can solve but also have the means to make a purchase. The author underlines that without leads, your products or services might as well not exist in the market. The profound importance of leads drives the book's main theme: generating a consistent stream of engaged leads is the key to building a thriving business.

The author also acknowledges the challenges and setbacks that entrepreneurs inevitably encounter on their journey to success. Rather than succumbing to adversity, he encourages readers to maintain hope, resilience, and the ability to adapt. He emphasizes that even in challenging situations, quick decision-making is crucial. Waiting or hesitating can result in missed opportunities, and thus, making calculated risks and executing prompt actions can lead to favorable outcomes.

Leveraging existing resources emerges as another critical principle. The author suggests that often, what you already have—such as skills, materials, or successful strategies—can be harnessed to create new income streams. By making the most of what's already available, entrepreneurs can accelerate their progress, achieve quicker results, and minimize costs.

Furthermore, the notion of maximizing profit potential is highlighted. Recognizing high-profit opportunities and focusing on revenue-generating activities that offer substantial returns can significantly contribute to both financial recovery and business growth. The author advocates for a strategic approach that prioritizes initiatives with the greatest potential for profitability.

Identify Your Offer: Write down the main product or service you're currently offering. Describe its key features, benefits, and how it solves a specific problem for your potential customers.

_____

_____

_____

_____

_____

_____

_____

_____

_____

_____

Craft an Irresistible Value Proposition: Imagine you have only one sentence to capture the essence of your offer. Write a value proposition that succinctly communicates the value your product or service brings to customers.

_____

_____

_____

_____

_____

_____

_____

_____

_____

_____

_____

_____

Create a Comparison Chart: Make a comparison chart that outlines how your offer differs from your competitors. Highlight the unique qualities that set your product or service apart.

Lesson 2:

Leads are the first step toward gaining more customers

Define Your Ideal Customer: Create a detailed persona of your ideal customer. Consider demographics, interests, pain points, and purchasing behavior. This will help you identify potential leads more effectively.

_____

_____

_____

_____

_____

_____

_____

_____

_____

_____

_____

_____

_____

_____

_____

_____

List Lead Sources: Make a list of platforms or channels where you can find potential leads. Include both online and offline sources, such as social media, industry events, email marketing, etc.

_____

_____

_____

_____

_____

_____

_____

_____

_____

_____

_____

_____

_____

_____

Craft a Lead Magnet: Design a lead magnet—a valuable resource that you can offer to potential leads in exchange for their contact information. It could be an e-book, a webinar, a checklist, or any other resource that aligns with your offer.

_____

_____

_____

_____

_____

_____

_____

_____

_____

_____

Lesson 3:

Facing Setbacks and Challenges

Reflect on Past Challenges: Recall a past setback or challenge you faced in your business journey. Write about how you approached the situation, the steps you took to overcome it, and the lessons you learned.

_____

_____

_____

_____

_____

_____

_____

_____

_____

_____

_____

_____

_____

_____

_____

_____

Create a Resilience Plan: Imagine a potential future challenge in your business. Write down three specific strategies you could implement to stay resilient and navigate through the challenge effectively.

_____

_____

_____

_____

_____

_____

_____

_____

_____

_____

_____

_____

_____

_____

_____

_____

Seek Inspiration: Research stories of successful entrepreneurs who faced significant setbacks but managed to turn their situations around. Write about the key takeaways from their experiences that resonate with you.

_____

_____

_____

_____

_____

_____

_____

_____

_____

Lesson 4:

Leveraging Existing Resources

Identify Unused Resources: List any skills, materials, or strategies you currently possess that could be repurposed or leveraged to create new income streams. Brainstorm potential ways to apply them differently.

_____

_____

_____

_____

_____

_____

_____

_____

_____

_____

_____

_____

_____

_____

_____

_____

Create a Resource Inventory: Make a comprehensive inventory of your existing resources, both tangible (equipment, tools) and intangible (skills, contacts). Determine how each resource can be utilized for new opportunities.

_____

_____

_____

_____

_____

_____

_____

_____

_____

_____

_____

_____

Innovative Combination: Experiment with combining two or more existing resources in a creative way to create a new product or service offering. Write down your idea and how it could address a specific customer need.

_____

_____

_____

_____

_____

_____

_____

_____

_____

Lesson 5:

Quick Decision-Making

Scenario Analysis: Imagine a time-sensitive business decision you need to make. Write down the pros and cons of each option, the potential risks involved, and the potential rewards. Make your decision based on your analysis.

_____

_____

_____

_____

_____

_____

_____

Create a Decision-Making Framework: Develop a simple decision-making framework that outlines the criteria you consider when making quick decisions. This could include factors like potential impact, alignment with goals, and available resources.

Role-Play Decision Scenarios: Enlist a friend or colleague to help you role-play various decision scenarios. Practice making quick decisions and explaining your reasoning in real-time. Reflect on how the role play went, and what you learned from it.

_____

_____

_____

_____

_____

_____

_____

Lesson 6:

Maximizing Profit Potential

Analyze Revenue Streams: List all the revenue streams currently generated by your business. Evaluate which streams have the highest profit margins and growth potential. Consider ways to expand or optimize them.

_____

_____

_____

_____

_____

_____

_____

_____

_____

_____

Identify High-Profit Opportunities: Brainstorm new product or service ideas that align with your existing expertise and customer base. Prioritize those that have the potential to generate substantial profits.

_____

_____

_____

_____

_____

_____

_____

_____

_____

_____

Value Proposition Enhancement: Choose one of your existing products or services. Write a short paragraph describing how you could enhance its value proposition to justify a higher price point, leading to increased profitability.

_____

_____

_____

_____

_____

_____

_____

_____

_____

_____

Lesson 7:

Focus on Lead Generation

Lead Generation Blueprint: Create a step-by-step plan for generating leads in your business. Outline specific actions you'll take, platforms you'll use, and a timeline for implementation.

_____

_____

_____

_____

_____

_____

_____

_____

_____

Lead Generation Metrics: Define key metrics to measure the effectiveness of your lead generation efforts. Write down how you'll track metrics like conversion rates, cost per lead, and lead quality.

_____

_____

_____

_____

_____

_____

_____

_____

Innovative Lead Generation Ideas: Brainstorm three unconventional strategies to attract leads. These could involve partnerships, collaborations, or tapping into emerging trends. Describe how you'd implement each idea.

_____

_____

_____

_____

_____

_____

_____

_____

_____

_____

_____

_____

_____

_____

_____

_____

_____

_____

_____

_____

_____

_____

_____

_____

_____

_____

_____

_____

Chapter 2: Focus on Engaged Leads

The chapter provides key takeaways that highlight the importance of engaged leads, learning from the market and others, authentic value delivery, audience-centric content, conversion pathways, effective lead magnet creation, core offer alignment, and the significance of clear calls to action (CTAs), urgency, and scarcity.

The chapter underscores the distinction between regular leads and engaged leads, highlighting the value of nurturing leads that exhibit interest in a product or service. Hormozi stresses the idea that engaged leads are more likely to convert and become paying customers, driving home the need to focus on this segment of the audience for better results.

Learning from market comparisons and case studies is recommended as a strategy to gain insights into effective advertising approaches. By observing what works for competitors and successful entrepreneurs, businesses can avoid unnecessary mistakes and expedite their advertising journey.

Authentic value delivery emerges as a core principle. Providing genuine value to potential leads through informative content or tangible solutions builds credibility and trust, forming a more meaningful connection between the business and its audience.

Crafting audience-centric content is pivotal in successful advertising. By tailoring lead magnets to align with the interests and needs of the target audience, businesses can significantly enhance lead engagement and conversion rates.

The concept of conversion pathways is introduced, focusing on the idea that lead magnets provide a pathway to the core offer. Lead magnets offer a solution to a specific problem, ultimately leading the engaged leads toward the main offer in a structured manner.

The chapter outlines a systematic approach to creating effective lead magnets. This involves identifying a problem, devising a solution, selecting delivery methods, testing and refining, ensuring ease of consumption, maintaining high quality, and encouraging future engagement.

Alignment with the core offer is emphasized as a critical factor in selecting the problem to address with a lead magnet. The chosen problem should be directly solvable using the core offer, creating a seamless transition from the lead magnet to the main offer.

The significance of CTAs is highlighted, providing clear instructions on the desired action and incorporating compelling reasons for immediate engagement. Urgency and scarcity are explored as psychological triggers that can effectively prompt action, and creative strategies for utilizing these triggers are discussed.

Engagement Assessment: Identify your existing leads and categorize them into regular leads and engaged leads based on their interactions with your content or products. Create a spreadsheet and list at least 20 leads, specifying their engagement behaviors. Reflect on patterns and trends to understand the characteristics of engaged leads.

_____

_____

_____

_____

_____

_____

_____

_____

_____

_____

Engagement Nurturing Plan: Develop a personalized engagement plan for your engaged leads. Create a sequence of valuable content, such as exclusive articles, webinars, or downloadable resources, that align with their demonstrated interests. Outline a 30-day engagement plan, including content topics and delivery methods.

_____

_____

_____

_____

_____

_____

_____

_____

_____

Engagement Tracking System: Set up a system to track engagement metrics. Choose key performance indicators (KPIs) like click-through rates, time spent on page, and social media interactions. Use tools like Google Analytics and social media insights to monitor and analyze these metrics regularly. Based on the results, make adjustments to your engagement strategy.

_____

_____

_____

_____

_____

_____

_____

Lesson 2:

Market Comparison and Learning from Others

Competitor Analysis: Select two of your main competitors and analyze their advertising strategies. Visit their websites, social media profiles, and ad campaigns. Create a comparative analysis chart highlighting their messaging, target audience, and unique selling propositions. Identify areas where your strategy can differentiate itself.

_____

_____

_____

_____

_____

_____

_____

Case Study Review: Research case studies of businesses in different industries that have successfully implemented lead engagement strategies. Choose three case studies and write a summary of each, highlighting the key takeaways and strategies they used. Identify how you can adapt and apply similar tactics to your own business.

_____

_____

_____

_____

_____

_____

_____

Strategy Implementation Plan: Develop an action plan for implementing the insights gained from competitor analysis and case studies. Outline specific changes you'll make to your current advertising approach, including revised messaging, new platforms to explore, and adjustments to your target audience. Set a timeline for each implementation step.

_____

_____

_____

_____

_____

_____

_____

_____

_____

Lesson 3:

Value Delivery and Authenticity

Value-Centric Content Creation: Brainstorm a list of informative and valuable content ideas that directly relate to your product or service. Choose three ideas from your list and outline a content plan for each, including the format (blog post, video, infographic), key points, and delivery schedule.

_____

_____

_____

_____

_____

_____

_____

Customer Testimonial Collection: Reach out to satisfied customers and request detailed testimonials or case studies that highlight the value they received from your offerings. Create a template for collecting these stories and outcomes, and craft personalized emails for reaching out to customers. Compile the collected testimonials into a dedicated section on your website.

_____

_____

_____

_____

_____

_____

_____

_____

Authenticity Check: Conduct a review of your current marketing materials, ensuring that your messaging aligns with the authentic value your business provides. Identify any instances of hype or exaggeration that could undermine your credibility. Rewrite these sections with a focus on transparency and accurate representation of your products or services.

_____

_____

_____

_____

_____

_____

_____

Lesson 4:

Audience-Centric Content

Audience Persona Creation: Develop detailed personas of your target audience segments. Include demographics, interests, pain points, and preferences. Use these personas to brainstorm content ideas that directly address their needs and desires.

_____

_____

_____

_____

_____

_____

_____

_____

_____

_____

Content Mapping: Create a content map that outlines the customer journey from awareness to conversion. Identify touchpoints where your audience interacts with your brand. For each touchpoint, plan relevant content that guides them towards the next stage in the journey.

_____

_____

_____

_____

_____

_____

Content Testing: Select one of your planned content pieces and create two different versions of it (e.g., blog post with different titles, video with different introductions). Use A/B testing to determine which version resonates better with your audience based on engagement metrics.

_____

_____

_____

_____

_____

_____

_____

_____

_____

_____

_____

Lesson 5:

Conversion Pathways

Lead Magnet Ideation: Brainstorm lead magnet ideas that address specific pain points of your audience. Choose one idea and create a detailed plan for its development, including the format (ebook, webinar, template), content outline, and design elements.

_____

_____

_____

_____

_____

_____

Pathway Design: Map out the customer journey from the initial engagement with your lead magnet to the eventual purchase of your core offer. Identify the steps in between and craft personalized email sequences or follow-up content that guides leads seamlessly through the pathway.

_____

_____

_____

_____

_____

_____

_____

_____

_____

_____

Pathway Testing: Implement your conversion pathway with a selected group of leads. Monitor their progress through the journey and gather feedback on their experience. Make necessary adjustments based on their interactions and responses.

_____
_____
_____
_____
_____
_____
_____
_____

Lesson 6:

Creating Effective Lead Magnets

Problem-Solution Brainstorming: List five common problems your target audience faces. Choose one problem and brainstorm potential solutions. Select the most feasible solution and outline the structure and content of a lead magnet that addresses this problem.

_____
_____
_____
_____
_____
_____
_____
_____
_____

Delivery Method Experimentation: Experiment with different delivery methods for your lead magnet. For example, if you're creating an ebook, consider offering it as a downloadable PDF, a series of web pages, or even an interactive presentation. Compare engagement and conversion rates across different delivery methods.

_____
_____
_____
_____
_____
_____
_____
_____

Quality Control Checklist: Develop a checklist for ensuring the quality of your lead magnets. Include items such as accurate information, professional design, ease of readability, and proper branding. Before publishing a new lead magnet, use the checklist to ensure all aspects are in order.

_____
_____
_____
_____
_____
_____
_____
_____
_____
_____
_____

Lesson 7:

Core Offer Alignment

Core Offer Mapping: Identify the core offer you want to promote and analyze its key features and benefits. Then, pinpoint a specific problem that your core offer can effectively solve. Craft a clear and concise statement that aligns the problem with your solution.

_____

_____

_____

_____

_____

_____

_____

_____

Offer-Problem Validation: Reach out to a few existing customers who have purchased your core offer and ask them about the specific problem they were looking to solve. Validate whether the problem you identified aligns with their needs and motivations for purchasing.

_____

_____

_____

_____

_____

_____

_____

_____

Value Proposition Refinement: Based on the feedback from customers and your analysis, refine the value proposition of your core offer. Ensure that it effectively communicates how your solution can solve the identified problem and deliver the desired outcomes.

_____

_____

_____

_____

_____

_____

_____

Lesson 8:

Clear Call to Action (CTA)

CTA Variation Creation: Choose a piece of content (e.g., a blog post, video) and create two different versions of the call to action. One should emphasize urgency, while the other highlights the value proposition. Monitor engagement metrics to determine which CTA performs better.

_____

_____

_____

_____

_____

_____

_____

_____

CTA Placement Experiment: Test different placements for your CTAs within your content. For instance, try placing a CTA at the beginning, middle, and end of a blog post. Compare click-through rates to identify the most effective placement for generating conversions.

CTA Language Crafting: Experiment with different wording and phrasing for your CTAs. Use action verbs, personalize the messaging, and highlight the benefits of taking action. Analyze the impact of these variations on conversion rates to refine your CTA language.

Lesson 9: Urgency and Scarcity

Limited-Time Offer Campaign: Design a limited-time offer for one of your products or services. Create a campaign that includes countdown timers, promotional emails, and social media posts emphasizing the urgency of the offer's expiration. Monitor the engagement and conversion rates during the campaign.

_____

_____

_____

_____

_____

Scarcity Showcase: Identify a product or service that has limited availability. Showcase the scarcity by clearly communicating the remaining quantity or time until it's no longer available. Monitor how this scarcity-focused messaging impacts customer inquiries and purchases.

_____

_____

_____

_____

_____

Urgency A/B Testing: Take an existing offer or product page and create two versions: one with urgency-focused messaging and one without. Monitor engagement metrics and conversion rates to determine whether urgency has a significant impact on driving immediate action.

_____

_____

_____

_____

_____

Chapter 3: Get Leads

In this section, "100m Leads" introduces a holistic strategy for effective outreach and conversion of potential customers. The approach is rooted in leveraging personal networks, cultivating authentic connections, and systematically scaling these efforts. The chapter underscores the importance of initiating warm outreach within one's existing personal network, utilizing resources such as email lists, phone contacts, and social media connections. The goal is to tap into a potential pool of leads already within reach, setting a foundation for business growth.

A central tenet is personalized communication, where crafting messages that genuinely resonate with each recipient is emphasized. By showing authentic interest and establishing connections based on available information, the strategy seeks to forge meaningful relationships. This approach aims to build trust and credibility without immediately focusing on transactions.

Consistent outreach is highlighted as a crucial practice. Engaging a substantial number of individuals daily, often around 100 contacts, is advocated. The strategy employs various communication channels, like phone calls, text messages, emails, and messaging platforms, to ensure persistent interaction. Following up up to three times within three days demonstrates respectful persistence, maximizing engagement without overwhelming recipients.

As business efforts expand, the chapter introduces the concept of scaling with systems. Automation tools and personnel are suggested to handle increased outreach volume effectively. Starting with personal outreach, this process evolves into a streamlined approach to engage larger audiences while maintaining communication quality.

Personal Contacts List: Create a comprehensive list of your personal contacts, including family, friends, colleagues, and acquaintances. Segment the list based on the strength of your relationship with each contact. Note down potential points of connection or shared interests for each person.

_____

_____

_____

_____

_____

Reach-Out Schedule: Develop a daily reach-out schedule for the next week. Decide which platform (email, social media, phone call) you'll use to contact each person. Allocate specific time slots for reaching out and stick to the schedule.

_____

_____

_____

_____

Connection Challenge: Challenge yourself to reach out to at least three people from your personal contacts list within the next 48 hours. Craft personalized messages for each, mentioning a shared memory or interest. Focus on building a genuine connection without discussing business initially.

_____

_____

_____

_____

Lesson 2:

Personalization and Connection

Contact Insights Research: Choose five people from your personal contacts list. Spend 15 minutes researching their social media profiles to gather insights into their interests, recent activities, and updates. Use this information to craft personalized messages that initiate meaningful conversations.

_____

_____

_____

_____

_____

Shared Experience Story: Recall a shared experience or memory you have with a particular contact. Write a short story that revolves around this experience and highlights the connection you share. Incorporate this story into your outreach message to create a warm and nostalgic feeling.

_____

_____

_____

_____

_____

_____

_____

_____

_____

Genuine Compliment Practice: Practice crafting genuine compliments that align with each contact's interests or achievements. Write down three compliments for different people. Use these compliments as conversation starters in your outreach messages.

_____

_____

_____

_____

_____

_____

Lesson 3:

Consistent Outreach

Daily Outreach Goal: Set a daily outreach goal for the next week. Determine the number of people you'll reach out to each day and the platforms you'll use. Create a visual tracker to monitor your progress and celebrate your achievements at the end of the week.

_____

_____

_____

_____

_____

_____

_____

_____

_____

_____

Follow-Up Sequence Creation: Develop a follow-up sequence template that you can use for contacts who haven't responded after your initial outreach. Outline the key points you'll cover in each follow-up message, maintaining a respectful and non-intrusive tone.

_____

_____

_____

_____

_____

_____

_____

Engagement Analysis: Review the responses and engagement you've received from your outreach efforts over the past two weeks. Identify any patterns in terms of response rates, preferred communication channels, and topics of interest. Use this analysis to refine your approach for higher engagement.

_____

_____

_____

_____

_____

_____

_____

_____

_____

_____

_____

Lesson 4:

Scaling with Systems

Outreach Process Documentation: Create a step-by-step document that outlines your current outreach process, including platform selection, message templates, and follow-up sequences. Review this document to identify areas where automation or delegation can be introduced as your business scales.

_____

_____

_____

_____

_____

Automation Tools Exploration: Research and explore automation tools suitable for managing warm outreach. Identify tools that can help schedule messages, track responses, and organize follow-ups. Select one tool to trial for the next week and assess its effectiveness.

_____

_____

_____

_____

_____

_____

_____

_____

_____

_____

Team Delegation Plan: Imagine your outreach workload has become too much for you to handle alone. Design a plan for delegating outreach tasks to a virtual assistant or team member. Include guidelines for maintaining a personalized touch and managing communication quality.

_____

_____

_____

_____

_____

_____

_____

Lesson 5:

ACA Framework for Effective Communication

Real-Life Application: Choose a recent conversation you had with a friend or family member. Reflect on how the ACA framework (Acknowledge, Connect, Ask) could have been applied to enhance the depth and quality of the conversation. Rewrite a portion of the conversation using the ACA approach.

_____

_____

_____

_____

_____

_____

_____

_____

Value-Oriented Scenario: Imagine you're reaching out to a potential lead who has shown interest in your industry. Craft an outreach message that follows the ACA framework while subtly introducing the value of your product or service. Focus on creating a balanced and engaging interaction.

_____

_____

_____

_____

_____

_____

Peer Feedback Session: Partner with a friend or colleague to practice the ACA framework in a role-play scenario. Take turns being the outreach initiator and recipient. Provide each other with constructive feedback on how well the framework was applied and areas for improvement.

_____

_____

_____

_____

_____

_____

_____

_____

_____

_____

_____

_____

_____

_____

Lesson 6:

Value Equation for Making Offers

Dream Outcome Exploration: Select one of your products or services and brainstorm the dream outcomes it can deliver for your customers. Write a short paragraph describing the emotional and practical benefits they would experience by using your offering.

Likelihood of Achievement Assessment: Assess the perceived likelihood of achieving the dream outcome for a specific product or service. On a scale of 1 to 10, rate how confident you are in its delivery. Write down at least three reasons that support your rating.

Time Delay and Effort Evaluation: Analyze the time delay and effort required for customers to achieve the dream outcome using your product or service. Create a comparison chart that highlights the advantages of your offering in terms of time saved and effort expended.

Lesson 7:

Creating an Irresistible Offer

Offer Elements Synthesis: Choose a product or service you offer and systematically address each element of the value equation (Dream Outcome, Likelihood of Achievement, Time Delay, Effort and Sacrifice). Write a persuasive paragraph that integrates all these elements to create an irresistible offer.

_____

_____

_____

_____

_____

_____

Customer Testimonial Integration: Collect a customer testimonial that aligns with one of the value elements (e.g., Dream Outcome achieved, Minimal Effort required). Incorporate this testimonial into an existing offer description to reinforce the perceived value.

_____

_____

_____

_____

_____

_____

Visual Representation: Create a visual representation of your offer that highlights the four value elements. This could be in the form of an infographic, flowchart, or comparison table. Use visuals to emphasize the benefits and outcomes your offer provides.

Lesson 8:

Transitioning from Free to Paid Offers

Offer Progression Strategy: Outline a step-by-step strategy for gradually transitioning a warm contact from a free offer to a paid product or service. Include touchpoints where you'll emphasize the value and benefits of upgrading to the paid offering.

_____

_____

_____

_____

_____

_____

_____

_____

_____

_____

Discount Graduation Plan: Develop a plan for offering discounts on your paid products or services as part of the transition process. Define the discount percentages and durations for each stage. Create an email template for announcing these limited-time discounts to your warm audience.

_____

_____

_____

_____

_____

_____

_____

_____

Free Offer Introduction: Design an introductory email that introduces a free resource or trial offer to a warm contact. Craft a compelling subject line and opening sentence that captures their attention and encourages them to explore the offer.

_____

_____

_____

_____

_____

_____

_____

_____

_____

_____

_____

_____

_____

_____

_____

_____

_____

_____

_____

_____

_____

_____

_____

_____

_____

_____

Post Free Content Part I

In this segment of "100m Leads" by Alex Hormozi, the author shares his personal journey of recognizing the power of building a substantial audience through free content. The narrative begins with the author's initial disbelief in the rapid success of individuals like Kylie Jenner and Dwayne Johnson, triggering a realization that a vast audience is a key driver of success. The author highlights the misconception that content itself is the asset; instead, it's the growing audience that holds value. Despite his skepticism, he acknowledges that a robust audience is a powerful tool for business growth and success. The author's transformation journey is underscored by his willingness to challenge and evolve his beliefs.

To learn the art of audience-building, the author invests in knowledge from an influencer with a successful audience. The advice includes consistent posting across various platforms, emphasizing the importance of volume in content creation. By following this guidance, the author experiences significant audience growth and engagement, which directly correlates with financial success.

The chapter delves into the strategy of posting free content to reach a wider audience efficiently. The content's value encourages sharing, expanding the warm audience further. The key benefit is that valuable content attracts engaged leads, resulting in successful offers and revenue.

However, the chapter also acknowledges the challenges of posting free content, such as difficulty in personalizing messages, competition, and the need for constant innovation. Despite these challenges, the chapter concludes that a larger, engaged audience leads to more lucrative opportunities.

The three components of audience-growing content are introduced: hook, retain, and reward. The chapter explains how these components work together to create a content unit, a fundamental element of effective content creation. Topics, formats, and the art of capturing attention are explored in detail to guide readers in crafting content that resonates with their audience.

Belief Reflection: Identify a belief or assumption you currently hold about audience growth and content creation. Reflect on where this belief originated and whether it aligns with the lessons from this section. Write a paragraph about how you can adapt or evolve this belief based on new insights.

_____

_____

_____

_____

_____

_____

_____

Mindset Shift Exercise: List three mindset shifts you can make to embrace the idea of audience building as a driver of success. For each shift, write a brief explanation of how it could positively impact your approach to content creation and audience engagement.

_____

_____

_____

_____

_____

_____

_____

_____

Contrasting Beliefs: Compare your initial beliefs about content creation and audience growth with the evolving beliefs discussed in this lesson. Create a visual chart or table that highlights the differences. Reflect on how adopting the new beliefs could lead to more effective content strategies.

Lesson 2:

Investing in Knowledge and Experience

Influencer Research Plan: Identify three influencers or experts in your industry who have achieved substantial audience growth. Research their content, strategies, and success stories. Create a research plan with specific questions to guide your investigation into their knowledge and experiences.

_____

_____

_____

_____

_____

Expert Interview Script: Imagine you have the opportunity to interview an influencer about their journey to building a substantial audience. Write down five insightful questions you would ask to gain valuable insights and lessons from their experiences.

_____

_____

_____

_____

_____

_____

_____

_____

_____

_____

_____

Learning Implementation Plan: Based on the knowledge and insights you've gained from influencers, outline three actionable steps you can take to accelerate your audience growth. Create a timeline for implementing these steps and track your progress over the next month.

_____

_____

_____

_____

_____

_____

Lesson 3:

Consistency and Volume

Content Calendar Creation: Develop a content calendar for the next month, specifying the types of content you'll post across various platforms. Allocate specific posting days and times for each piece of content. Stick to this calendar and track engagement metrics to assess its impact.

_____

_____

_____

_____

_____

_____

_____

_____

_____

_____

Platform Diversity Strategy: Choose two social media platforms you currently use or plan to use. Research how influencers successfully post content consistently on both platforms. Write down three strategies for adapting your content to each platform's unique features while maintaining consistency.

_____

_____

_____

_____

_____

_____

Content Posting Experiment: Experiment with posting frequency on a chosen platform. For one week, post content at different times of the day and analyze engagement metrics. Based on the results, identify the posting schedule that generates the highest engagement and implement it in your content calendar.

_____

_____

_____

_____

_____

_____

_____

_____

_____

_____

_____

_____

Lesson 4:

Content's Role in Audience Growth

Audience Engagement Analysis: Select one of your recent content pieces that received significant engagement. Identify the top three engagement metrics (likes, comments, shares) and the audience's demographic information. Write a brief analysis of how this engagement contributes to audience growth.

_____

_____

_____

_____

_____

Content Sharing Strategy: Develop a plan for encouraging your engaged audience to share your content with their networks. Create a template for sharing posts and messages that resonates with your audience's values and motivations. Implement this strategy in your next content post.

_____

_____

_____

_____

_____

_____

_____

_____

_____

Engagement-to-Lead Conversion Plan: Outline a step-by-step plan for converting engaged followers into warm leads. This could involve offering a valuable lead magnet in exchange for their contact information. Map out the communication sequence and follow-up emails to nurture these leads towards making a purchase.

_____

_____

_____

_____

_____

_____

Lesson 5:

Audience Growth and Engagement

Audience Growth Goal Setting: Define a clear audience growth goal for the next three months. Determine the percentage increase you want to achieve in your social media followers, email subscribers, or other relevant metrics. Break down this goal into monthly targets.

_____

_____

_____

_____

_____

_____

_____

_____

_____

_____

Engagement Analysis Challenge: Choose a recent piece of content and analyze the engagement metrics. Identify areas where engagement could have been improved. Write a mini action plan with three strategies you can implement in your next content post to enhance engagement.

_____

_____

_____

_____

_____

Engagement Feedback Loop: Create a feedback loop with your audience by asking for their input on your content. Craft a post or email asking followers for suggestions or topics they'd like you to cover. Use this feedback to tailor your content to their preferences and interests.

_____

_____

_____

_____

_____

_____

_____

_____

_____

_____

_____

Lesson 6:

Formatting for Familiarity

Platform Research: Choose a social media platform you use frequently. Research the most popular content formats and styles on that platform. Create a checklist of the visual and structural elements that your content should include to align with your audience's expectations.

_____

_____

_____

_____

_____

Content Adaptation Practice: Take a piece of content you've previously posted on one platform and adapt it for a different platform. Apply the formatting and style preferences specific to that platform while maintaining the core message of your content.

_____

_____

_____

_____

_____

_____

_____

_____

_____

_____

Content A/B Testing: Choose a content format (e.g., video, info-graphic, long-form article) and create two versions of the same content using different formatting techniques. Post both versions on different platforms and track engagement metrics to determine which format resonates better with your audience.

_____

_____

_____

_____

_____

Lesson 7:

Value Per Second

Content Value Assessment: Select one of your recent content pieces and evaluate its value using the "value per second" concept. Estimate how much value your audience gains for the time they invest in consuming the content. Write a short paragraph reflecting on whether the content meets this value standard.

_____

_____

_____

_____

_____

_____

_____

_____

_____

_____

_____

_____

Content Engagement Analysis: Choose a high-engagement content piece and analyze the retention rate. Calculate the percentage of viewers who stayed engaged until the end. Identify the factors that contributed to their sustained interest and brainstorm ways to replicate this in future content.

_____

_____

_____

_____

_____

_____

Segmented Value Analysis: Divide your audience into two segments based on their engagement level (highly engaged vs. less engaged). Choose a content piece and assess its value per second for each segment. Write a reflection on whether the content effectively addresses the varying needs of both segments.

_____

_____

_____

_____

_____

_____

_____

_____

Lesson 8:

Matching Expectations

Content Promise Review: Select three recent content posts and review the promises or hooks you used to attract your audience. Analyze whether the content delivered on these promises and exceeded audience expectations. Write down specific instances where you successfully matched or exceeded expectations.

_____

_____

_____

_____

_____

Expectation Alignment Exercise: Choose a content piece and list three clear expectations you believe your audience might have before engaging with the content. Write a paragraph for each expectation explaining how the content addresses and fulfills these expectations.

_____

_____

_____

_____

_____

Pre-Content Engagement Prompt: Experiment with using a pre-content engagement prompt that primes your audience's expectations before they consume your content. Develop a prompt that generates curiosity or sets the context for the upcoming content. Monitor engagement metrics to assess its impact.

_____

_____

_____

_____

#2 Post Free Content Part II

In this excerpt from "100m Leads" by Alex Hormozi, the author delves into the strategy of monetizing a warm audience, emphasizing a balance between offering value and making strategic asks. The chapter outlines the "give-give-give, give-give-give, until they ask" approach, underscoring the importance of providing substantial value to the audience before making monetization requests. The author introduces the concept of "give until they ask," which encourages audience members to initiate engagement by expressing interest in offers.

The section examines the dynamics of the "give : ask" ratio, where providing valuable content surpasses promotional content to maintain audience trust and engagement. The television advertising model and Facebook's content-to-advertisement ratio are discussed as reference points for achieving a healthy give-ask balance.

Strategies for integrating and intermittently including promotional content within free content are explored. The author emphasizes the need to maintain audience goodwill while incorporating promotion strategically to avoid diminishing trust and impeding growth.

The chapter introduces two approaches for scaling audience growth: the depth-then-width approach and the width-then-depth approach. The former involves maximizing one platform before moving to others, while the latter focuses on establishing a presence on multiple platforms and then expanding content depth. The importance of adapting content to the platform's format is highlighted to maximize reach and efficiency.

The significance of content creation as a complementary strategy to paid advertising is emphasized through the author's personal experience. By nurturing demand with valuable free content, businesses can enhance their returns on all advertising methods. The chapter concludes by stressing the value of sharing personal experiences and stories to connect with the audience, as well as focusing on specific niches to establish authority.

Content Audit and Ratio Calculation: Review your last 10 content pieces (e.g., blog posts, videos, social media posts). Calculate the ratio of "give" content (value-driven content) to "ask" content (promotional or call-to-action content). Write down the ratio for each piece and reflect on whether it aligns with the "give-give-give, give-give-give, until they ask" principle.

_____

_____

_____

_____

Value-Driven Content Brainstorm: Brainstorm five value-driven content ideas that provide immediate benefits or solutions to your audience's pain points. Select one idea and create a content outline that emphasizes value delivery without a direct ask or promotion.

_____

_____

_____

_____

Reciprocity Experiment: Experiment with the "give-give-give" strategy by creating a content series focused solely on delivering value without making any asks. Monitor engagement metrics and audience feedback to assess the impact of this approach on building goodwill and engagement.

_____

_____

_____

_____

_____

_____

Lesson 2:

"Give Until They Ask" Strategy.

Value-Driven Engagement Plan: Develop a 30-day engagement plan that revolves around delivering consistent value to your audience. Create a schedule of daily or weekly value-driven content posts, such as tips, insights, or mini-tutorials. Track engagement metrics and note any increase in audience inquiries or interaction.

_____

_____

_____

_____

_____

Engagement-Driven Conversion Case Study: Research a case study of an influencer or business that successfully implemented the "give until they ask" strategy. Summarize the key steps they took to build engagement and trust before making offers. Identify how you can apply similar steps to your own content strategy.

_____

_____

_____

_____

_____

_____

_____

_____

Audience Feedback Collection: Create a survey or feedback form and share it with your audience. Ask them about their preferences for content types, topics, and engagement levels. Use their responses to tailor your content to their preferences and align with the "give until they ask" approach.

_____

_____

_____

_____

_____

_____

Lesson 3:

Scaling Strategies

Platform Prioritization Strategy: Choose one social media platform where you're currently active. Determine whether the "depth-then-width" or "width-then-depth" strategy aligns better with your audience and goals. Write a paragraph explaining your chosen strategy and how you plan to maximize its impact.

_____

_____

_____

_____

_____

_____

_____

_____

_____

Cross-Platform Value Integration: If you're using multiple platforms, choose a piece of value-driven content and adapt it for different platforms. Maintain the core message while tailoring the format and style to each platform's audience. Post the adapted content and compare engagement metrics.

_____

_____

_____

_____

_____

New Platform Launch Plan: Imagine you're planning to expand to a new social media platform. Create a step-by-step launch plan that outlines how you'll introduce yourself, establish your content style, and build engagement on the new platform. Include a timeline for achieving specific growth milestones.

_____

_____

_____

_____

_____

_____

_____

_____

_____

_____

_____

Lesson 4:

Share Your Experience

Personal Story Reflection: Reflect on a significant personal experience or challenge you've overcome in your journey. Write a personal story that captures the lessons you learned and how they relate to your expertise. Craft this story in a way that resonates with your audience's emotions and aspirations.

_____

_____

_____

_____

_____

_____

Experience-Sharing Content Strategy: Choose a recent value-driven content piece and brainstorm ways to incorporate your personal experience or story into it. Develop a plan for infusing authenticity and relatability into your content while delivering valuable insights.

_____

_____

_____

_____

_____

_____

_____

_____

_____

_____

_____

Audience Connection Through Stories: Share a relatable personal experience in a piece of content, such as a blog post or video. Encourage your audience to share their own stories in the comments. Engage with their stories and create a sense of community through shared experiences.

_____

_____

_____

_____

_____

_____

Lesson 5:

Narrow Content Focus

Niche Expertise Exploration: Choose a specific niche or topic within your industry that aligns with your expertise. Research the current demand and competition for content in this niche. Write a brief paragraph explaining why this niche resonates with your knowledge and passion.

_____

_____

_____

_____

_____

_____

_____

_____

Narrow-to-Broad Content Evolution: List three subtopics within your chosen niche. Create a content plan that gradually expands from narrow topics to broader themes over the course of three months. Outline the specific content pieces you'll create for each subtopic.

_____

_____

_____

_____

_____

_____

_____

Credibility Building Case Study: Research a case study of an influencer or brand that started with a narrow content focus and gradually expanded to broader topics. Summarize their journey and the impact it had on their credibility and audience engagement. Reflect on how you can apply a similar approach.

_____

_____

_____

_____

_____

_____

_____

_____

_____

_____

_____

_____

_____

Cold Outreach:

The author delves into a significant turning point in their journey, marked by the challenges posed by the COVID-19 pandemic. As businesses were grappling with uncertainty, the author's companies faced unprecedented adversity. A substantial portion of their customer base went out of business, protests raged across various platforms, and political promises permeated the atmosphere. Against this backdrop of turmoil, the author's companies—Gym Launch, Prestige Labs, and ALAN—relied on brick-and-mortar establishments that were forcibly shut down due to the pandemic. Adding to their predicament, even their paid ads took a hit after a software update by Apple.

Caught in the maelstrom of these events, the author found themselves wrestling with a series of daunting questions. How could they sustain the business amidst such uncertainty? What was the extent to which they should tap into their personal accounts or life savings? The author's internal conflict, stemming from a lack of direction in such dire circumstances, was palpable.

One Saturday morning, a message from a potential candidate named Cale brought a glimmer of hope. Cale had expressed his eagerness to work for the author, and while the author had initially rejected his application due to an apparent lack of need for salesmen, the situation had changed. A conversation was initiated, which revealed Cale's background in a gym software company that solely relied on cold outreach for leads. This sparked the author's interest, as the company was generating a staggering $10,000,000 per month through this strategy alone.

Despite doubts about whether the cold outreach system could be adapted to their context, the author struck a deal with Cale, giving him the opportunity to develop and execute the cold outreach strategy. The months that followed were a series of ups and downs, marked by successes and failures in the cold outreach process. This journey led them from zero sales in September to generating millions per month through cold outreach.

The author extracted valuable lessons from this experience: the realization that another company in their space was thriving, despite their initial beliefs about market size; the impact of private advertising on competitors' success; the potential of building a profitable cold outreach machine; the significance of setting proper expectations for the scaling process; and the advantage of working with someone experienced in the specific strategy.

This chapter further delves into the mechanics of cold outreach, outlining a step-by-step approach. It begins by explaining the challenges strangers introduce to the process, including the lack of contact information, being ignored, and encountering disinterest. The solution, the author explains, entails three steps: establishing a means of contact, formulating compelling messages to capture attention, and persistently reaching out until the recipient is receptive.

The importance of trust-building is emphasized, as cold outreach inherently involves approaching strangers who lack familiarity with the business. Despite these challenges, the author underscores that successful cold outreach involves overwhelming leads with upfront value to spark their interest. The concept is presented as a numbers game, where the more outreach efforts are made, the higher the engagement potential becomes.

Personal Perspective Shift: Reflect on your current view of cold outreach. Write a short paragraph about any reservations or doubts you have about this strategy. Then, list three potential benefits you can see from embracing cold outreach as a lead generation method.

_____

_____

_____

_____

_____

_____

Benefits Visualization: Create a vision board or collage that illustrates the positive outcomes you anticipate from successful cold outreach. Include images or words that represent increased leads, engagement, and ultimately, business growth. Display this visualization in your workspace.

Case Study Analysis: Research and analyze a case study of a business that successfully utilized cold outreach to generate leads. Summarize the key elements of their approach and the results they achieved. Write a reflection on how their success story inspires you to implement cold outreach.

_____

_____

_____

_____

_____

_____

_____

_____

_____

Lesson 2:

Step-by-Step Approach

Lead Criteria Brainstorm: Identify the ideal criteria for your target leads based on your business objectives. List demographic, psychographic, and behavioral characteristics that align with your product or service. Use this list as a foundation for building your targeted lead list.

_____

_____

_____

_____

_____

_____

Message Crafting Practice: Choose a lead from your list and craft a cold outreach message tailored to their needs and interests. Write a concise message that highlights the value you can provide and encourages engagement. Review and refine the message for clarity and impact.

_____

_____

_____

_____

_____

_____

_____

_____

_____

_____

Multi-Channel Engagement Plan: Develop a week-long engagement plan for a selected lead. Outline how you will reach out to them through different channels (email, LinkedIn, social media). Include specific dates and times for each outreach attempt and track responses received.

_____

_____

_____

_____

_____

_____

Lesson 3:

Build a Targeted List

Lead Criteria Brainstorm: Identify the specific criteria that your ideal leads should meet. Include demographic, psychographic, and behavioral factors. Write a paragraph explaining why each criterion is important for your business.

_____

_____

_____

_____

_____

_____

_____

_____

_____

_____

List Building Method Exploration: Research and outline at least three different methods for building a targeted lead list. Describe the advantages and disadvantages of each method. Choose one method you're most inclined to use and explain why.

_____

_____

_____

_____

_____

_____

_____

Personalized List Building Plan: Design a step-by-step plan for building a targeted lead list using a combination of methods. Include the tools or resources you'll need for each step. Set a timeline for completing each phase of list building.

_____

_____

_____

_____

_____

_____

_____

_____

_____

_____

_____

_____

_____

Lesson 4:

Craft Compelling Messages

Audience Empathy Practice: Choose a hypothetical lead from your targeted list. Write a brief description of their characteristics, challenges, and goals. Use this information to draft a message that demonstrates your understanding of their needs.

_____

_____

_____

_____

_____

Message A/B Testing: Create two variations of a cold outreach message for different segments of your targeted list. Experiment with tone, length, and value proposition. Send the messages and track which version receives higher engagement.

_____

_____

_____

_____

_____

_____

_____

_____

_____

_____

_____

_____

Message Customization Exercise: Select a lead from your targeted list. Craft a cold outreach message that addresses their specific pain points and interests. Highlight how your product or service can provide a solution. Review the message for clarity and impact.

_____

_____

_____

_____

_____

_____

_____

Lesson 5:

Focus on Trust Building

Trust-Building Storytelling: Recall a personal or professional experience that demonstrates your expertise or commitment to providing value. Write a short storytelling piece that incorporates this experience into a cold outreach message. Focus on building trust through authenticity and relatability.

_____

_____

_____

_____

_____

_____

_____

_____

Initial Value Proposition: Choose a lead from your list and identify a way to provide immediate value to them without asking for anything in return. Craft an outreach message that offers this value upfront, showcasing your willingness to contribute before seeking engagement.

_____

_____

_____

_____

_____

_____

Value Showcase Plan: Create a plan to deliver consistent value to your leads over the course of a month. Outline the types of content, resources, or insights you'll share through your outreach efforts. Monitor engagement metrics and track how value delivery influences responses.

_____

_____

_____

_____

_____

_____

_____

_____

_____

_____

_____

Lesson 6:

Flexibility in Targeting

Ideal Customer Profile Definition: Define your ideal customer profile by combining the lead criteria you identified earlier. Describe this profile in detail, including demographic details, pain points, and aspirations. Use this profile as a reference when selecting leads for outreach.

_____

_____

_____

_____

_____

Segmented Outreach Strategy: Choose two distinct segments within your ideal customer profile. Develop a strategy for reaching out to each segment with tailored messages that address their specific needs. Compare engagement rates between the two segments to identify effective approaches.

_____

_____

_____

_____

_____

_____

_____

_____

_____

Niche Approach Experiment: Select a niche or industry segment within your target audience. Craft a cold outreach message that speaks directly to the unique challenges and opportunities faced by this niche. Monitor the response rate to determine the effectiveness of niche-specific messaging.

_____

_____

_____

_____

_____

_____

Lesson 7:

Deliver Big Fast Value

Lead Magnet Creation: Develop a lead magnet that provides substantial value to your target leads. Choose a topic that addresses a common pain point or challenge. Write a brief outline of the content, such as an eBook or guide, and include a call-to-action that encourages leads to engage.

_____

_____

_____

_____

_____

_____

_____

_____

Value Showcase Calendar: Create a content calendar for showcasing valuable resources over the next month. Include a mix of lead magnets, blog posts, videos, or other content formats. Plan your cold outreach messages around the content you're sharing to align with the "big fast value" principle.

_____

_____

_____

_____

_____

_____

_____

Value Measurement Experiment: Test the impact of delivering value on engagement rates by sending a message to a lead that includes a valuable resource without a direct ask. Track the response rate and any subsequent interactions or engagement to assess the effectiveness of this approach.

_____

_____

_____

_____

_____

_____

_____

_____

_____

_____

_____

_____

Lesson 8:

Persistent Follow-Up

Follow-Up Sequence Design: Develop a follow-up sequence that spans two weeks for a specific lead. Outline the content and messaging for each follow-up attempt, incorporating different communication channels (email, LinkedIn, phone). Implement this sequence and monitor response patterns.

_____

_____

_____

_____

_____

_____

Engagement Timeline Reflection: Choose a lead you successfully engaged through persistent follow-up. Reflect on the engagement timeline and note the touchpoints where they showed increased interest or responsiveness. Write a brief analysis of how consistent follow-up played a role in their engagement.

_____

_____

_____

_____

_____

_____

_____

_____

Customized Follow-Up Plan: Customize your follow-up approach for different segments within your target audience. Outline how the messaging and frequency of follow-ups might differ based on factors such as lead source, industry, or engagement history.

_____

_____

_____

_____

_____

_____

Lesson 9:

Secrecy and Competitive Edge

Outreach Privacy Assessment: Evaluate your current cold outreach methods in terms of privacy and confidentiality. Write down any measures you've taken to keep your outreach strategies hidden from competitors. Identify additional steps you can take to enhance the secrecy of your approach.

_____

_____

_____

_____

_____

_____

_____

_____

_____

_____

_____

Competitive Analysis Task: Research a competitor in your industry and analyze their lead generation strategies. Write a brief comparison of their public strategies versus the privacy-oriented approach of cold outreach. Reflect on the potential advantages of keeping your methods confidential.

_____

_____

_____

_____

_____

_____

Competitor Unawareness Strategy: Imagine you've successfully generated leads through cold outreach. Develop a plan for showcasing your business's growth without revealing the specific strategies you used. Craft a communication message or content piece that highlights your accomplishments without divulging confidential information.

_____

_____

_____

_____

_____

_____

_____

_____

_____

_____

_____

_____

Lesson 10:

Reliable Scalability

Outreach Volume Projection: Estimate the number of outreach attempts required to achieve a specific lead generation goal. Consider factors like response rates, engagement rates, and your desired number of leads. Create a visual representation of how outreach attempts correlate with lead generation.

_____

_____

_____

_____

_____

_____

Outreach Progression Timeline: Create a timeline for gradually scaling your outreach efforts over a six-month period. Specify the increase in outreach attempts, leads generated, and responses received at each stage. Track your actual progress against this timeline and adjust as needed.

_____

_____

_____

_____

_____

_____

_____

_____

Outreach ROI Calculation: Calculate the return on investment (ROI) for your cold outreach efforts based on the leads generated and the revenue generated from these leads. Compare this ROI with other lead generation methods you've used. Write a reflection on the predictability and scalability of cold outreach.

_____

_____

_____

_____

_____

_____

_____

_____

_____

_____

_____

_____

_____

_____

_____

_____

_____

_____

_____

_____

_____

_____

_____

_____

Run Paid Ads Part I

The author explores the intricacies of maximizing the effectiveness of paid advertisements. The central premise revolves around honing in on the right audience to ensure efficient ad campaigns. Instead of questioning whether ads work, the focus shifts to optimizing their impact. The process involves finding a balance between expenditure and customer conversion. Similar to cold outreach, paid ads target audiences with lower trust levels, necessitating strategies to capture their interest.

Efficiency is achieved by presenting the offer to as many potential customers as possible, overcoming the challenge of profitability when the right audience isn't reached. The goal is to refine the audience gradually, moving from a global reach to a narrower, engaged pool. This progression includes selecting an appropriate platform, utilizing available targeting methods, tailoring the ad to repel unwanted viewers, and prompting the remaining audience to take action.

The chapter emphasizes that successful advertising requires a platform where the four key elements are present: a personal understanding of the platform, the ability to target the ideal audience, familiarity with platform-specific ad formatting, and the budget to accommodate ad placement costs. These principles remain consistent despite evolving platforms.

The author delves into the "What-Who-When Framework," which guides ad content creation. This involves identifying the value proposition (What), understanding the target audience's perspective (Who), and communicating relevant timing (When) to align with audience needs.

Key takeaways include the importance of capturing attention through effective callouts, both verbal and nonverbal. Callouts range from broad to hyper-specific, aiming to engage the right people while standing out amid noise. The author advises answering potential audience questions within the ad to enhance engagement.

Audience Persona Creation: Identify your target audience for a specific product or service. Develop a detailed persona including demographics, interests, pain points, and online behavior. Write a paragraph describing how this audience aligns with your offering.

_____

_____

_____

_____

_____

_____

Audience Refinement Plan: Choose a broad audience segment and outline a plan to gradually refine your targeting. Define the criteria you'll use to narrow down the audience over time. Monitor engagement metrics to assess the impact of each refinement.

_____

_____

_____

Efficiency Metrics Analysis: Select a recent ad campaign and analyze the efficiency metrics such as click-through rate (CTR), conversion rate, and cost per click (CPC). Reflect on how these metrics relate to audience targeting and ad messaging.

_____

_____

_____

_____

_____

_____

_____

Lesson 2:
Balancing Specificity and Scale

Specificity vs. Scale Debate: Write a comparative analysis of the advantages and disadvantages of highly specific targeting versus broad audience targeting in paid ads. Discuss scenarios where each approach is most suitable and how to find a balance between the two.

_____

_____

_____

_____

_____

Resource Allocation Plan: Imagine you have limited resources for ad spend. Develop a plan that outlines how you'll allocate your budget between ads with specific targeting and those with broader appeal. Justify your allocation strategy based on potential ROI.

_____

_____

_____

_____

_____

_____

_____

_____

_____

_____

Early Wins Strategy: Choose a specific product or service and design an ad campaign with highly specific targeting to achieve early wins. Outline the audience criteria, messaging, and expected outcomes. Reflect on how these wins can fuel future campaigns.

_____

_____

_____

_____

Lesson 3:

Ad Crafting

Value Proposition Statement: Select a product or service and craft a value proposition statement that concisely communicates its benefits and unique selling points. Use this statement as a foundation for ad messaging and test it in your campaigns.

_____

_____

_____

Ad Message Simplification Exercise: Choose a recent ad you've run and identify any unnecessary details or complexity in the message. Rewrite the ad copy to convey the same value proposition with increased clarity and simplicity.

_____

_____

_____

_____

_____

_____

Ad Copy A/B Testing: Create two variations of ad copy for the same product, each focusing on a different aspect of its value. Run these variations as A/B tests in separate campaigns and compare their performance in terms of engagement and conversion.

_____

_____

_____

_____

_____

_____

_____

Lesson 4:

Risk and Reward

ROI Calculation Practice: Calculate the return on investment (ROI) for a recent ad campaign by considering the total revenue generated from conversions and the total ad spend. Reflect on how this ROI compares to your initial goals and expectations.

_____

_____

_____

_____

_____

_____

_____

_____

_____

_____

_____

Profit Margin Analysis: Choose a product or service you're advertising and calculate the profit margin for each sale. Create a chart that illustrates how the profit margin changes as your ad spend increases. Reflect on the balance between profit and investment.

_____

_____

_____

_____

_____

Scaling Impact Scenario: Imagine doubling your ad spend for a successful campaign. Write a brief analysis of the potential impact on overall revenue, taking into account both increased sales and higher ad costs. Discuss the risk-reward trade-off in scaling.

_____

_____

_____

_____

_____

_____

_____

_____

_____

_____

_____

_____

_____

_____

_____

_____

Lesson 5:

Attention-Grabbing Callouts

Attention-Grabbing Ad Scenario: Design an ad campaign for a new product launch. Develop an attention-grabbing callout that captures the audience's interest within the first few seconds. Describe the visual and verbal elements you'd use to achieve this.

_____

_____

_____

_____

_____

Callout Evolution Analysis: Select two of your past ads—one with a broad appeal and another with a specific callout. Compare their engagement metrics and analyze how the callouts contributed to the audience's response.

_____

_____

_____

_____

_____

_____

_____

_____

_____

_____

_____

_____

Callout Variation Experiment: Take an existing ad and create three different versions with varying callouts: one broad, one specific, and one curiosity-driven. Run these versions as separate campaigns and analyze which callout type performs best.

_____

_____

_____

_____

_____

_____

Lesson 6:

The What-Who-When Framework

Product Value Exploration: Select a specific product or service from your business. Identify its key value propositions and benefits using the "What" element of the framework. Write a short paragraph describing how these value propositions address customer needs.

_____

_____

_____

_____

_____

_____

_____

_____

_____

_____

_____

Timely Experience Identification: Consider the timing at which your product or service provides the most value to customers. Write a brief description of a scenario or event that aligns with this timing. Integrate this scenario into the "When" element of your ad content.

_____

_____

_____

_____

_____

_____

_____

Target Audience Analysis: Choose an ideal customer persona for the chosen product. Write a fictional profile that includes demographics, pain points, and aspirations. Use this persona to craft the "Who" element of your ad content.

_____

_____

_____

_____

_____

_____

_____

_____

_____

_____

_____

_____

_____

Lesson 7:

Speak to Audience Questions

Frequently Asked Questions Compilation: Compile a list of common questions customers ask about your product or service. Choose three questions that are most relevant to your audience. Craft a short paragraph answering each question concisely.

_____

_____

_____

_____

_____

_____

Customer Testimonial Integration: Choose a customer testimonial that addresses a common concern or question. Write an ad that includes this testimonial and frames it in a way that responds to the audience's potential queries.

_____

_____

_____

_____

_____

_____

_____

_____

_____

_____

_____

_____

Audience Question Anticipation: Think from the perspective of a potential customer encountering your ad. Identify at least two questions they might have about your offering. Write an ad message that addresses these questions upfront.

_____

_____

_____

_____

_____

_____

Lesson 8:

Use of Visual and Auditory Cues

Visual Elements Brainstorm: List visual elements (images, icons, colors) that are associated with your brand or product. Choose a specific product and design an ad with visually appealing elements that align with its attributes.

_____

_____

_____

_____

_____

_____

_____

_____

_____

_____

Audience Reaction Analysis: Choose an ad with visual and auditory cues that you've run in the past. Analyze user comments and engagement metrics to understand how these cues affected audience perception and interaction.

_____

_____

_____

_____

_____

_____

Verbal and Nonverbal Contrast: Compare two different ads—one with a strong verbal callout and another with a strong visual callout. Write a reflection on how the combination of verbal and nonverbal cues in each ad influences its impact.

_____

_____

_____

_____

_____

_____

_____

_____

_____

_____

_____

_____

_____

_____

_____

Run Paid Ads Part II:

The primary theme revolves around the intricacies of successful paid advertising strategies. The author places a strong emphasis on prioritizing efficiency over creativity when it comes to crafting and managing ad campaigns. This signifies a shift from focusing solely on eye-catching and inventive advertisements to concentrating on measurable and meaningful results. A central concept introduced in this chapter is the LTGP to CAC ratio, a crucial metric that holds the key to gauging the efficiency of paid ads. This ratio involves comparing the Lifetime Gross Profit (LTGP) generated from a customer to the Cost to Acquire a Customer (CAC). The author asserts that a healthy advertising strategy should ideally yield an LTGP to CAC ratio greater than 3 to 1. This benchmark not only indicates profitability but also provides a clear insight into how well an ad campaign is performing in terms of the actual returns generated relative to the costs incurred.

The author underscores the significance of distinguishing between issues related to sales conversion and those connected to advertising effectiveness. They assert that if potential customers are showing interest, have the capacity to make a purchase, yet aren't converting, the problem might lie more in the sales process or product offerings rather than the efficacy of the ads themselves. This distinction is pivotal in troubleshooting and addressing the right areas for improvement. The chapter also recommends a strategic approach to entering the realm of paid advertising. The author advises against rushing into paid advertising without a solid foundation. Instead, they propose exploring and maximizing other revenue-generating methods like partnerships, organic content, and email marketing before fully committing resources to paid ads. This approach not only establishes a more sustainable revenue base but also provides valuable insights and experience that can inform future ad strategies.

Efficiency Assessment: Review your previous paid ad campaigns. Identify one campaign where creativity overshadowed efficiency and another where efficiency was the main focus. Compare the outcomes and write a reflection on how efficiency impacted the results.

_____

_____

_____

_____

_____

Efficiency-Creativity Balance: Choose a product or service to advertise. Write a paragraph discussing how you can strike a balance between efficiency and creativity in your ad strategy. Outline specific ways you can ensure that efficiency remains the primary focus.

_____

_____

_____

_____

_____

Efficiency Improvement Plan: Select a recent ad campaign that lacked efficiency. Create a plan to improve its efficiency while maintaining its effectiveness. Consider adjustments in targeting, messaging, and optimization techniques.

_____

_____

_____

_____

_____

_____

_____

_____

Lesson 2: LTGP to CAC Ratio

LTGP and CAC Calculation: Calculate the lifetime gross profit (LTGP) for a typical customer and the cost to acquire a customer (CAC) for a recent ad campaign. Compare these values and reflect on how they contribute to the LTGP to CAC ratio.

_____

_____

_____

_____

_____

_____

Optimizing LTGP: Identify at least two ways you can increase the lifetime value of a customer, such as upselling, cross-selling, or subscription models. Write a paragraph explaining how these strategies can positively impact the LTGP to CAC ratio.

_____

_____

_____

_____

_____

_____

_____

_____

_____

_____

_____

CAC Reduction Strategy: Outline a plan to lower the cost to acquire a customer (CAC) for a specific product or service. Consider optimization techniques, improved targeting, and efficient ad spend allocation. Discuss how this reduction can improve the overall ad strategy.

_____

_____

_____

_____

_____

_____

_____

Lesson 3:
Don't Confuse Sales and Advertising Problems

Engaged Leads Analysis: Choose a product or service and analyze the characteristics of your engaged leads. Write a paragraph discussing how to identify whether a lack of sales is due to advertising inefficiency or potential sales conversion issues.

_____

_____

_____

_____

_____

_____

_____

_____

_____

Sales Conversion Assessment: Select a recent ad campaign that generated engaged leads but had low sales conversion rates. Develop a checklist of factors to evaluate whether the issue lies in the advertising or the sales process.

_____

_____

_____

_____

_____

_____

Collaborative Solution: Imagine a scenario where your sales team identifies a conversion issue. Write a brief script for a collaborative meeting between your advertising and sales teams to address the challenge and find a solution together.

_____

_____

_____

_____

_____

_____

_____

_____

_____

_____

_____

_____

_____

_____

Lesson 4:
Start with the Other Methods First

Prioritization Matrix: List various customer acquisition methods, including partnerships, organic content, email marketing, and paid ads. Create a matrix to rank them based on initial investment required and potential return. Justify why paid ads should be approached later.

_____

_____

_____

_____

_____

_____

_____

_____

_____

_____

_____

_____

_____

_____

_____

_____

_____

_____

_____

_____

_____

Alternative Methods Experiment: Choose an alternative method, such as partnerships or email marketing, and create a plan to execute it for a specific product. Implement the plan and document the results to illustrate its effectiveness compared to paid ads.

_____

_____

_____

_____

_____

_____

_____

_____

_____

_____

_____

_____

_____

_____

_____

_____

_____

_____

_____

_____

_____

_____

_____

Sequential Strategy Design: Design a sequential strategy for a new product launch. Outline the order in which you'll implement various customer acquisition methods, starting from methods with lower investment and gradually moving towards paid ads.

Core Four On Steroids

The chapter begins by addressing the common misconception among entrepreneurs that they have reached the limits of their market potential. This limited mindset hampers growth, preventing them from exploring untapped opportunities for generating more leads.

The author introduces the concept of the "Core Four" advertising strategies: warm reach outs, content posting, cold reach outs, and paid ads. These strategies serve as the foundation for attracting and engaging potential customers, allowing entrepreneurs to maximize lead generation.

The "More Better New" framework is presented as a pivotal strategy for lead generation improvement. It involves three stages: doing more of what's already effective, enhancing existing strategies, and exploring new platforms or methods. This iterative process ensures continuous growth by progressively optimizing advertising efforts.

The Rule of 100 is introduced as a principle to drive consistent action. This rule dictates performing 100 primary actions daily for 100 consecutive days across all core four activities. Following this rule ensures a steady stream of engaged leads and consistent progress toward growth goals.

Continuous testing and improvement are highlighted as essential components of successful lead generation. The author emphasizes identifying constraints within each strategy, pinpointing drop-off points where potential leads are lost. These constraints serve as areas for improvement, allowing entrepreneurs to refine their approaches effectively.

The importance of expanding to new placements and platforms is stressed after maximizing existing strategies. The author encourages entrepreneurs to venture beyond their comfort zones, exploring different platforms, placements, and core four activities. This expansion opens avenues to reach previously untapped audiences, resulting in increased lead generation and business growth.

Market Expansion Mindset Shift: Reflect on your current business and identify any assumptions you've made about market saturation. Write a paragraph challenging these assumptions and exploring potential avenues for growth that you might have overlooked.

_____

_____

_____

_____

_____

_____

Untapped Niche Exploration: Choose a specific niche or segment within your market. Research and write a short proposal on how you can expand your reach to this untapped audience, outlining strategies to attract their attention and generate leads.

_____

_____

_____

_____

Growth Mindset Journal: Create a journal for a week to document instances where you encounter challenges related to lead generation. For each challenge, write down two potential solutions that align with the idea that there's always room for growth.

_____

_____

_____

_____

_____

_____

_____

Lesson 2:
Core Four Advertising Strategies

Strategy Depth Analysis: Choose one of the core four strategies (warm reach outs, posting content, cold reach outs, running paid ads) that you've used before. Reflect on how deeply you've explored and executed this strategy. Write a plan to take it to its fullest potential.

_____

_____

_____

_____

_____

_____

_____

Comprehensive Strategy Map: Create a visual map that illustrates how the core four strategies work together in generating leads. Describe the synergy between each strategy and write a short narrative explaining how they complement each other.

_____

_____

_____

_____

_____

_____

_____

_____

_____

Strategy Integration Challenge: Select two of the core four strategies and brainstorm innovative ways to integrate them for lead generation. Write a short scenario detailing how the combination of these strategies can enhance engagement and conversion rates.

_____

_____

_____

_____

_____

Lesson 3:
"More Better New" Framework

Current Strategy Enhancement: Choose one of the core four strategies that you're currently using. Write a paragraph outlining how you can apply the "more better new" framework to improve this strategy. Highlight specific areas where you can do more, do it better, or explore new methods.

_____

_____

_____

_____

_____

_____

_____

_____

_____

_____

Strategy Reflection and Adjustment: Evaluate a recent lead generation campaign you conducted. Write a reflection on what went well, what could be improved, and how you can apply the "more better new" framework to adjust your approach for better results.

_____

_____

_____

_____

_____

_____

_____

Testing New Platforms: Research and identify a new platform or method within your industry that you haven't utilized before. Write a plan on how you can integrate this new element into your lead generation efforts, including the benefits it offers.

_____

_____

_____

_____

_____

_____

_____

_____

_____

_____

_____

_____

_____

Lesson 4:
Rule of 100

Personalized Rule of 100 Plan: Customize the Rule of 100 for your business. Choose one of the core four strategies and create a daily plan that outlines the specific actions you'll take to achieve the Rule of 100. Document how this consistent effort impacts lead generation.

_____

_____

_____

_____

_____

_____

_____

Progress Tracking Journal: Implement the Rule of 100 for warm reach outs for 30 days. Create a journal to record your daily actions, progress, and the outcomes you observe. Reflect on the trends you notice and whether this consistent effort boosts lead generation.

_____

_____

_____

_____

_____

_____

_____

_____

_____

_____

_____

Rule of 100 Challenge: Challenge a friend or colleague to join you in implementing the Rule of 100 for a specific core four strategy. Create a shared document where you both track your daily actions and outcomes. Compare results and insights at the end of the challenge.

_____

_____

_____

_____

_____

_____

_____

Lesson 5:
Continuous Testing and Improvement

Constraint Identification Exercise: Review your recent lead generation efforts across the core four strategies. Identify one or two specific points where leads tend to drop off or engagement decreases. Develop a plan to test and improve these areas.

_____

_____

_____

_____

_____

_____

_____

_____

Testing Hypothesis Generation: Choose a core four strategy and generate three hypotheses for improvements you can test. Write a brief description of each hypothesis and how you plan to implement and measure the changes.

_____

_____

_____

_____

_____

_____

_____

Data-Driven Strategy Adjustment: Analyze the data from a recent lead generation campaign and identify the top-performing elements. Write a reflection on how you can leverage these successful aspects to improve other campaigns within the core four strategies.

_____

_____

_____

_____

_____

_____

_____

_____

_____

_____

_____

_____

_____

_____

Lesson 6:
Expanding to New Placements and Platforms

Platform Exploration Plan: Research a new platform or placement relevant to your industry that you haven't used before. Write a plan on how you can adapt one of the core four strategies to this platform to attract a fresh audience and generate leads.

_____

_____

_____

_____

_____

_____

_____

Cross-Strategy Adaptation: Choose a core four strategy that you've found successful. Imagine how you can adapt this strategy to a completely different placement or platform. Write a brief scenario illustrating how this adaptation can lead to growth.

_____

_____

_____

_____

_____

_____

_____

_____

_____

Audience Expansion Proposal: Develop a proposal for expanding your reach through a new placement or platform. Outline the potential benefits, target audience, and specific strategies you would employ to engage this new audience and generate leads.

_____

_____

_____

_____

_____

_____

_____

_____

_____

_____

_____

_____

_____

_____

_____

_____

_____

_____

_____

_____

_____

_____

_____

_____

Chapter 4:
#1 Customer Referrals - Word of Mouth

The chapter begins with a personal anecdote about the author's experience with customer referrals, highlighting the transformative impact of word of mouth in business growth. The author's journey from a challenging financial situation to becoming a multi-millionaire emphasizes the significance of satisfied customers sharing their positive experiences with others.

The author reflects on a moment when an advertising campaign was unintentionally halted, causing a temporary dip in sales. However, the steady influx of leads and sales continued due to strong word of mouth referrals from satisfied customers. This incident underscored the value and influence of customer referrals in driving consistent business growth.

A pivotal moment at a speaking engagement with gym owners solidified the author's understanding of the power of word of mouth. Asking the audience how many learned about the author's business through other gym owners revealed the substantial impact of referrals, with a significant portion of attendees raising their hands. This event highlighted the exponential growth potential of referrals.

The chapter delves into the mechanics of how referrals work, emphasizing that referrals occur when engaged leads are sent to a business by referrers, often satisfied customers. The focus is on obtaining more referrals from existing customers, as these tend to be more valuable and cost-effective for business growth.

Referrals are presented as a dual benefit for business growth. First, referrals contribute to higher lifetime gross profits (LTGP), as referred customers tend to purchase more expensive items more frequently. Second, referrals reduce customer acquisition costs (CAC), as customers referring others incur no additional cost to the business.

The exponential nature of word of mouth referrals is highlighted, showcasing how one satisfied customer can lead to a cascading effect of new customers. The concept of exponential growth through referrals is contrasted with linear growth observed in other advertising methods.

Mini-Win Action Plan: Select a recent customer interaction and identify a smaller, achievable win you can provide within the first few days. Write an action plan detailing how you will deliver this win and communicate it to the customer.

_____

_____

_____

_____

_____

_____

Progress Report Template: Design a progress report template that highlights achievements and milestones related to your product or service. Create a mock progress report and imagine how this positive update would impact customer satisfaction.

_____

_____

_____

_____

48-Hour Success Story: Craft a fictional success story highlighting a customer's positive experience within the first 48 hours of their purchase. Describe the scenario, emotions, and outcomes to emphasize the importance of creating a lasting impression early on.

_____

_____

_____

_____

_____

_____

Lesson 2:
Decrease Effort and Sacrifice for Customers

Customer Journey Analysis: Map out the typical customer journey from initial contact to post-purchase. Identify pain points where customers might experience effort or sacrifice. Write a plan to address these challenges and make the journey smoother.

_____

_____

_____

_____

_____

_____

_____

_____

Product Improvement Brainstorm: Choose a product or service feature and brainstorm ways to make it more convenient for customers. Write a short proposal outlining how these improvements will reduce customer effort and enhance their experience.

_____

_____

_____

_____

_____

_____

_____

_____

Feedback-Driven Improvement: Design a feedback collection form that encourages customers to provide insights about their experience. Use this data to create an action plan for continuous improvement based on the common issues raised.

_____

_____

_____

_____

_____

_____

Lesson 3:
Call To Action - Continue Selling

Product Expansion Ideas: Select a product or service you offer and brainstorm three potential upgrades or complementary products. Write a marketing pitch for each idea, highlighting the benefits of these additional offerings to existing customers.

_____

_____

_____

_____

_____

_____

_____

_____

_____

_____

_____

Value Reinforcement Email: Draft an email that reminds customers of the value they've gained from their initial purchase. Incorporate persuasive language to encourage them to explore new products or upgrades that align with their preferences.

_____

_____

_____

_____

_____

_____

_____

_____

_____

Customer Engagement Calendar: Design a calendar that outlines opportunities for engaging existing customers throughout the year. Include seasonal promotions, exclusive offers, and product launches tailored to their interests and needs.

_____

_____

_____

_____

_____

_____

_____

_____

_____

_____

_____

Lesson 4:
Asking for Referrals as an Offer

Referral Program Integration Plan: Choose a product or service and outline how you can integrate a referral program as part of the purchase process. Write a step-by-step plan detailing how customers and their friends can participate.

_____

_____

_____

_____

_____

_____

_____

Value Proposition for Referrals: Craft a compelling value proposition that explains the benefits of referring others to your products or services. Write a short script for an elevator pitch that communicates these benefits effectively.

_____

_____

_____

_____

_____

_____

_____

_____

_____

_____

Innovative Referral Strategy: Research innovative referral strategies used by companies in different industries. Write a concept paper that proposes how you can adapt one of these strategies to your business model to boost customer referrals.

_____

_____

_____

_____

_____

_____

_____

Lesson 5:
Referral Strategies - Seven Approaches

Referral Benefit Experiment: Choose one-sided or two-sided referral benefits for a specific product or service. Write a plan to test both approaches and compare the results in terms of referral engagement and success.

_____

_____

_____

_____

_____

_____

_____

_____

_____

Referral Timing Scenario: Imagine a scenario where a customer has just made a purchase. Write a dialogue where you explain the benefits of referrals and encourage them to refer a friend immediately after their purchase.

_____

_____

_____

_____

_____

_____

_____

Referral Event Proposal: Develop a proposal for a referral event that encourages customers to refer others. Outline the event details, rewards, and promotional strategies you would use to maximize participation.

_____

_____

_____

_____

_____

_____

_____

_____

_____

_____

_____

_____

_____

_____

Lesson 6:
Monetize Goodwill by Giving Value

Value-Centric Marketing Message: Choose a product or service and write a marketing message that emphasizes the value you deliver and the impact it has on customers. Focus on creating goodwill through value-centric language.

_____

_____

_____

_____

_____

_____

Goodwill Building Plan: Outline a 30-day plan to build goodwill with your existing customers. Include actions like sending personalized thank-you messages, offering surprise bonuses, and providing valuable content to enhance their experience.

_____

_____

_____

_____

_____

_____

_____

_____

_____

Long-Term Value Visualization: Create a visual representation of how delivering consistent value today translates into long-term benefits, including customer referrals. Use this visualization to convey the concept of monetizing goodwill to your audience.

#2 Employees

The section introduces the concept of lead-getting employees as individuals trained to acquire leads for a business using the same methods the owner used to acquire leads initially. These employees engage in activities such as running ads, creating content, and outreach to bring in leads.

The author emphasizes that lead-getting employees offer several benefits: they contribute to increased engaged leads for the business while reducing the workload on the owner. By trading managing for doing, business owners can achieve more with less time and effort.

Two scenarios are presented to illustrate the impact of lead-getting employees on business success. In Scenario #1, the business owner works extensively to generate profit, resembling a high-paying job. In contrast, Scenario #2 highlights a business that operates without the owner's constant involvement, making it a valuable asset.

The wealth-building potential of lead-getting employees is discussed. When a business runs successfully without the owner's continuous input, it transforms into an attractive investment for potential buyers. This shift from a liability reliant on the owner to an asset that generates income independently increases the business's overall value.

The author reflects on past misconceptions about employees, such as the belief that "nobody can do it but me." This mindset hindered growth as the author attempted to outcompete employees. The shift in perspective towards acknowledging that everyone is replaceable and that tasks can be done better by others enabled the author to focus on more strategic activities.

The "Internal Core Four" approach is introduced as a method to attract employee leads. By adapting the core four lead generation strategies used for customers, businesses can effectively communicate job openings and opportunities to potential employees.

Collaboration Vision Board: Create a vision board that represents the concept of collaboration in achieving long-term success. Include images, quotes, and keywords that illustrate the value of teamwork. Write a reflection on how this vision aligns with your business goals.

_____

_____

_____

Collaboration Brainstorm: List three potential collaborative projects or initiatives that your business could undertake to achieve larger goals. Detail the roles and responsibilities of team members for each project and describe how collaboration will lead to better outcomes.

_____

_____

_____

_____

Collaborative Success Story: Write a fictional success story that highlights a scenario where effective teamwork led to a significant achievement. Describe the roles played by different team members, the challenges they overcame together, and the positive impact on the business.

_____

_____

_____

_____

_____

_____

_____

_____

Lesson 2:
Identifying Challenges

Failure Analysis Report: Imagine a situation where your business faces a sales goal failure similar to the one described in the book. Write a detailed analysis of the failure, identifying potential underlying issues, and suggest steps to address them proactively.

_____

_____

_____

_____

_____

_____

Root Cause Exploration: Choose a challenge your business has encountered recently and conduct a root cause analysis. Use the "5 Whys" technique to dig deeper into the issue and uncover the true reasons behind the challenge.

_____

_____

_____

_____

_____

_____

_____

_____

_____

_____

_____

Assumption vs. Reality Exercise: List three assumptions you currently hold about your business's success. Research and gather data to validate or challenge these assumptions. Write a reflection on how challenging assumptions can lead to a better understanding of your business's trajectory.

_____

_____

_____

_____

_____

Lesson 3:
Addressing Churn and Hiring

Employee Churn Impact Assessment: Imagine a scenario where your business is facing high employee churn rates. Assess the potential impact of this issue on your sales goals and overall business performance. Write a plan to address and mitigate the effects of churn.

_____

_____

_____

_____

_____

_____

_____

_____

_____

_____

_____

Hiring Process Improvement: Evaluate your current hiring process and identify one area that could be improved to attract and retain top talent. Write a step-by-step plan for implementing this improvement, including ways to identify candidates who align with your business values.

_____

_____

_____

_____

_____

Churn Reduction Strategy: Develop a strategy to reduce employee churn based on the challenges highlighted in the book. Write an action plan that includes mentorship programs, feedback loops, and initiatives to create a positive work environment.

_____

_____

_____

_____

_____

_____

_____

_____

_____

_____

_____

_____

_____

_____

Lesson 4:
Scale Through Employees

Scaling Readiness Checklist: Create a checklist to assess your business's readiness to scale through hiring employees. Include criteria such as workload, processes, and revenue goals. Write a reflection on whether your business is prepared for this growth phase.

_____

_____

_____

_____

_____

_____

Employee Role Definition: Choose a key role that you would need to hire for as your business scales. Write a detailed job description, including responsibilities, qualifications, and desired skills. This exercise will help clarify the value employees bring to your team.

_____

_____

_____

_____

_____

_____

_____

_____

_____

_____

_____

_____

Scaling Strategy Brainstorm: Brainstorm three strategies for effectively scaling your business through hiring employees. Write a brief overview of each strategy, including the potential benefits and challenges of implementation.

_____

_____

_____

_____

_____

_____

Lesson 5:
Employee Training and Replication

Training Manual Creation: Choose a specific task or process within your business that you want employees to replicate. Write a comprehensive training manual that follows the "Document, Demonstrate, Duplicate" approach. Include step-by-step instructions and visual aids.

_____

_____

_____

_____

_____

_____

_____

_____

_____

Employee Training Simulation: Design a training simulation exercise for a new employee. Create a scenario where they need to replicate a task based on the training manual you've developed. Write a description of the simulation and its learning objectives.

_____

_____

_____

_____

_____

_____

Training Feedback Loop: Develop a feedback loop that encourages employees to provide input on the training materials and processes. Write a plan for regular check-ins, surveys, or focus groups to ensure the training is effective and adaptable.

_____

_____

_____

_____

_____

_____

_____

_____

_____

_____

_____

_____

_____

_____

Lesson 6:
Calculating ROI and Employee Leads

Employee ROI Calculation: Choose a specific lead-getting employee or team and calculate the ROI of their efforts. Write down their monthly payroll costs and compare them to the number of engaged leads they generate. Analyze the efficiency of their contributions.

_____

_____

_____

_____

_____

_____

Employee Performance Dashboard: Create a dashboard template that tracks key performance metrics of lead-getting employees. Include metrics such as lead conversion rates, engagement rates, and ROI. Write a reflection on how this dashboard can provide actionable insights.

_____

_____

_____

_____

_____

_____

_____

_____

_____

_____

ROI Improvement Strategy: Imagine that you want to enhance the ROI of your lead-getting employees. Write a strategy that outlines how you will optimize their performance by investing in training, tools, or process enhancements.

_____

_____

_____

_____

_____

_____

_____

_____

_____

_____

_____

_____

_____

_____

_____

_____

_____

_____

_____

_____

_____

_____

_____

_____

#3 Agencies

The author reflects on their past experiences with agencies, highlighting a common cycle of excitement, initial results, deteriorating performance, and eventual cancellation. These experiences lead to the realization that agencies can play a valuable role in business growth, but not in the conventional way they often advertise.

The author shares their journey of learning how to use agencies effectively, emphasizing the importance of avoiding pitfalls and learning from past mistakes. They express a desire to help others avoid wasting money and instead channel those resources towards learning and growth.

The concept of investing in agencies as a means to learn new methods and platforms is introduced. The author suggests that agencies can provide a shortcut to profitability by leveraging their expertise and avoiding the trial-and-error process.

The author outlines how they now use agencies in a strategic manner. They enter agency relationships with a defined purpose and a set timeframe. Instead of relying solely on agencies, the author seeks to understand the processes and decisions driving their success, aiming to eventually transition to a consulting arrangement.

A strategy is introduced where two agencies are sequentially employed. The first agency is engaged to learn the fundamentals of a new platform, and then a more advanced agency is brought in to optimize and maximize results. This method allows for both immediate results and long-term skill development.

A checklist for selecting the right agency is provided, including factors such as word-of-mouth referrals, associations with prominent companies, a clear sales process, focus on long-term strategy, transparent communication, proven track record, and realistic expectations.

The author highlights the idea that investing in agency services involves trading money for important skills that may not be readily available elsewhere. Learning from agencies accelerates growth and efficiency by avoiding costly trial-and-error processes.

Skepticism Analysis: Reflect on a situation where you were initially skeptical about investing in a new method or strategy for your business. Describe the reasons for your skepticism and how it influenced your decision-making. Write down any potential missed opportunities due to this skepticism.

_____

_____

_____

_____

_____

Value of Learning Investment: Think about a recent instance where you invested time and resources to learn about a new advertising method or platform. Write a journal entry describing the knowledge and skills you gained from this investment and how they contributed to your business growth.

_____

_____

_____

_____

_____

_____

Skepticism Challenge: Choose a current advertising method or strategy that you're skeptical about. Write down three ways you could research and gather information to overcome your skepticism and make an informed decision about its potential value.

_____

_____

_____

_____

_____

_____

Lesson 2:
Optimal Agency Utilization

Agency Expertise Inventory: Create a list of advertising methods, platforms, or strategies that you'd like to learn more about. Research and identify agencies specializing in these areas. Write a brief summary of what each agency can offer in terms of expertise and learning potential.

_____

_____

_____

_____

_____

Benefits of Agency Expertise: Write a short essay on the advantages of hiring an agency to learn new advertising methods efficiently. Include examples of how agencies' experience and expertise can accelerate your learning curve and lead to better outcomes.

_____

_____

_____

_____

_____

_____

_____

_____

_____

_____

_____

_____

Learning Plan Creation: Choose one advertising method you'd like to learn from an agency. Write a step-by-step learning plan that includes goals, milestones, timelines, and a budget for hiring the agency. This plan will help you structure your learning investment effectively.

_____

_____

_____

_____

_____

Lesson 3:
Purposeful Agency Relationship

Agency Relationship Strategy: Imagine you're planning to hire an agency to learn a new skill or method. Write a detailed outline of your purpose for hiring the agency, your desired learning outcomes, and how you envision transitioning to a consulting arrangement once you've gained proficiency.

_____

_____

_____

_____

_____

_____

_____

_____

_____

_____

_____

Transition Roadmap: Design a roadmap for transitioning from a full agency relationship to a consulting arrangement. Write down the steps you'll take to gradually reduce your reliance on the agency's services while maintaining the knowledge and skills you've acquired.

Reflection on Skill Mastery: Reflect on a time when you mastered a new skill or method with the help of an agency. Write a personal narrative that describes the journey from initial learning to achieving proficiency. Include the challenges you faced, the agency's role, and the benefits of skill mastery.

Lesson 4:
Balancing Agency Attention

Agency Sequence Strategy: Choose an advertising platform you're interested in exploring. Write a plan for sequentially hiring two agencies—one competent and another elite—to guide your learning journey. Describe how each agency's expertise will contribute to your short-term and long-term goals.

_____

_____

_____

_____

_____

Agency Role Play: Assume the role of a business owner seeking to balance agency attention. Write a dialogue between yourself and two agencies—one focusing on basics and another on advanced strategies. Explore how their expertise aligns with your learning needs.

_____

_____

_____

_____

_____

_____

_____

_____

_____

_____

Parallel Learning Experiment: Experiment with parallel learning by exploring a new advertising platform simultaneously with the help of a competent agency and self-guided learning. Document your experiences, compare progress, and reflect on the effectiveness of both approaches.

_____

_____

_____

_____

_____

_____

_____

Lesson 5:
Selecting the Right Agency

Agency Selection Checklist: Create a checklist for evaluating and selecting the right agency for your learning needs. Include criteria such as referrals, company associations, communication style, track record, and long-term strategy focus. Use this checklist for future agency decisions.

_____

_____

_____

_____

_____

_____

_____

_____

_____

Agency Scouting Journal: Research agencies in your industry and compile a journal of potential candidates. Write brief profiles for each agency, highlighting their strengths, weaknesses, and alignment with your learning goals. Use this journal as a reference for future agency partnerships.

_____

_____

_____

_____

_____

_____

Agency Assessment Simulation: Simulate an agency assessment process by analyzing a fictional agency's capabilities. Write a critique of their sales process, communication style, transparency, and track record. Use this exercise to practice evaluating agencies objectively.

_____

_____

_____

_____

_____

_____

_____

_____

_____

_____

_____

_____

_____

Lesson 6:
Progression and Cost-Efficiency

Learning Investment ROI Calculation: Choose a specific advertising method or platform you've learned through an agency. Calculate the ROI of your learning investment by comparing the costs of agency services with the benefits gained from improved outcomes. Write a reflection on the financial value of your investment.

_____

_____

_____

_____

_____

_____

_____

Skill Transition Plan: Create a skill transition plan that outlines how you'll surpass an agency's capabilities and achieve better results in-house. Write down the steps you'll take to gradually reduce your reliance on agency expertise while maintaining high-quality outcomes.

_____

_____

_____

_____

_____

_____

_____

_____

_____

Cost-Efficiency Strategy: Write a strategy for optimizing the cost-efficiency of your learning investments over time. Detail how you'll balance agency expenses with in-house skill development and identify scenarios where the benefits of self-guided learning outweigh agency costs.

#4 Affiliates and Partners

The author delves into the concept of leveraging affiliates as a potent means of lead generation for businesses. Affiliates, which are essentially independent entities, are introduced as valuable partners who promote your products or services to their existing audience in exchange for commissions or rewards. This partnership can lead to a substantial increase in engaged leads and customers for your business.

The section advocates for the creation of what the author terms an "affiliate army." This involves a strategic process of recruiting, activating, and integrating affiliates into your marketing strategy. Each affiliate added to your arsenal introduces a new channel through which you can reach potential customers, thus fostering rapid and scalable growth for your business.

One of the key strategies highlighted is the implementation of a tiered payout structure. This structure is designed to incentivize affiliates based on their performance. By offering varying levels of commissions or rewards, you encourage affiliates to strive for higher levels of engagement and sales. Additionally, the chapter suggests that affiliates invest in your product or achieve a certain level of expertise, aligning their success with the success of your business. This deeper commitment increases the likelihood of sustained efforts and long-term collaboration.

A particularly intriguing concept discussed is the "multi-step process upsell." This strategy involves affiliates offering the initial step of a multi-step product or service for free. By doing so, customers are enticed to engage with the first stage, creating a sense of value and anticipation for subsequent steps. This approach not only fosters customer loyalty but also facilitates the upselling of further stages, leading to increased revenue.

In essence, the section underscores the transformative potential of affiliates as a high-leverage means of obtaining leads. By skillfully building an affiliate network, implementing a tiered payout structure, ensuring affiliate investment, and guiding customers through a multi-step process, businesses can tap into a dynamic source of growth and customer acquisition. This strategic approach transforms affiliates from mere partners to essential components of a business's lead generation and scaling strategy.

Affiliate Potential Assessment: Identify potential affiliates within your industry or niche who could promote your products. Create a list of at least five potential affiliates, detailing their audience size, reach, and relevance to your offerings.

_____

_____

_____

_____

_____

_____

Affiliate Collaboration Pitch: Write a sample pitch email or message to approach a potential affiliate. Introduce yourself, explain the mutual benefits of collaboration, and outline how their audience could benefit from your products. Use this template to initiate conversations with potential affiliates.

_____

_____

_____

_____

Affiliate Research and Analysis: Select a successful business that utilizes affiliates. Research their affiliate program, commission structure, and the types of rewards they offer. Write an analysis of how their approach aligns with the high-leverage lead-getting concept and how you can adapt similar strategies.

_____

_____

_____

_____

Lesson 2:
Affiliate Army for Scaling

Affiliate Recruitment Strategy: Design a strategy for recruiting affiliates effectively. Create a step-by-step plan that outlines how you'll identify potential affiliates, approach them, and integrate them into your marketing strategy. This plan will serve as your guide for building an affiliate army.

_____

_____

_____

_____

_____

_____

Scaling with Affiliates Simulation: Imagine your business has just added a new affiliate who is driving significant leads and sales. Write a reflective journal entry on how this addition has impacted your business's growth and how you plan to leverage this affiliate to achieve rapid scalability.

_____

_____

_____

_____

_____

_____

_____

_____

_____

Affiliate Activation Plan: Write a checklist of actions you'll take to activate and engage new affiliates once they join your program. Include steps such as providing marketing materials, hosting orientation sessions, and offering ongoing support to ensure their success.

_____

_____

_____

_____

_____

Lesson 3:
Tiered Payout Structure

Tiered Payout Structure Design: Create a tiered payout structure for your affiliate program based on performance levels. Outline different commission rates or rewards for affiliates who achieve specific lead generation and sales targets. This structure will motivate affiliates to excel.

_____

_____

_____

_____

_____

_____

_____

_____

_____

_____

_____

Effective Payout Communication: Develop a communication plan to inform affiliates about the tiered payout structure. Write a series of emails or messages that explain the new structure, highlight its benefits, and offer guidance on how affiliates can maximize their earnings through increased engagement.

_____

_____

_____

_____

_____

_____

_____

_____

Affiliate Performance Comparison: Compare the performance of two affiliates—one who receives flat commissions and another who benefits from a tiered payout structure. Write a comparative analysis of their engagement, leads generated, and sales driven to understand the impact of the tiered structure.

_____

_____

_____

_____

_____

_____

_____

_____

_____

_____

_____

Lesson 4:
Investment and Qualification

Affiliate Investment Proposal: Craft a proposal outlining how affiliates can invest in your product or become certified experts. Explain the benefits of their investment, such as deeper product understanding, increased credibility, and alignment with your business goals.

_____

_____

_____

_____

_____

_____

Affiliate Success Stories: Research and compile success stories of affiliates who invested in your product or became certified experts. Write brief profiles that highlight their achievements, impact on your business, and the ways their commitment led to sustained engagement.

_____

_____

_____

_____

_____

_____

_____

_____

_____

Affiliate Investment Benefits Essay: Write an essay discussing the benefits of having invested affiliates. Include insights into how their commitment translates into higher lead quality, improved customer relationships, and long-term loyalty. Use this essay to reinforce the importance of alignment with affiliates' success.

Lesson 5:
One Step In A Multi-Step Process Upsell

Multi-Step Upsell Scenario Creation: Imagine a scenario where you offer the first step of a multi-step process through affiliates. Write a short script or dialogue between an affiliate and a potential customer, highlighting the value of the free step and building anticipation for subsequent steps.

Upsell Messaging Optimization: Develop a messaging strategy for upselling subsequent steps of the multi-step process to customers who have completed the free step. Write a series of emails or messages that emphasize the benefits, outcomes, and value of the next steps.

_____

_____

_____

_____

_____

_____

_____

Upsell Conversion Analysis: Analyze the conversion rates of customers who completed the free step through affiliates and subsequently purchased the remaining steps. Write a reflection on the effectiveness of this approach in increasing upsell conversions and its impact on overall revenue.

_____

_____

_____

_____

_____

_____

_____

_____

_____

_____

_____

_____

Chapter 5: Get Started

In Chapter 5, the author delves into the principles and mindset required to succeed in building a robust advertising strategy. The chapter begins by emphasizing that true success takes time and persistence, debunking the notion of "overnight success." Drawing from personal experience, the author shares that their own journey to reaching a net worth of $100M took over a decade of consistent effort and dedication.

The central concept introduced is the analogy of the "Many Sided Die." This analogy serves as a framework for understanding the iterative nature of advertising success. Just as in a game where players roll dice to hit a green side, advertisers need to continuously test and learn, rolling the metaphorical advertising dice repeatedly to hit upon successful strategies. Regardless of the initial conditions (number of sides), with enough trials, everyone has a chance at success.

The author emphasizes that the key to success lies in persistent action and continuous testing. They provide a summary of the strategies covered in the book, which include defining leads, turning leads into engaged leads, utilizing the Core Four advertising methods (reaching out to acquaintances, posting publicly, approaching strangers, and running paid ads), maximizing these methods for effectiveness, leveraging the Four Lead Getters (Customers, Employees, Agencies, and Affiliates), and applying rules like the "Rule of 100" and "Open to Goal" when advertising in the real world.

Additionally, the author shares insights about scaling and adapting advertising efforts. They stress the importance of understanding constraints and finding ways to overcome them to maximize growth. The principle of continuous refinement is crucial, as advertisers must evolve their strategies by building on what works and adjusting what doesn't.

Overall, the chapter encapsulates the mindset shift necessary for successful advertising. It emphasizes that the path to success is not about the specific circumstances one starts with, but rather about the commitment to learning, testing, and iterating. By embracing the analogy of the "Many Sided Die," advertisers can better understand the iterative nature of success and approach their advertising endeavors with a long-term perspective, allowing for growth and improvement over time.

Mindset Assessment and Shift Plan: Reflect on your current mind-set towards advertising and lead generation. Identify any limiting beliefs that may be holding you back. Create a plan to shift your mindset towards an aggressive and proactive approach, setting specific goals and strategies to adopt a growth-oriented mindset.

_____

_____

_____

_____

Budget Expansion Strategy: Develop a strategy for tripling your advertising budget like the speaker did. Outline the steps you'll take to assess your current budget, determine the additional investment required, and allocate funds to different advertising channels or strategies.

_____

_____

_____

_____

_____

Shift Reflection Journal: Start a journal where you document your mindset shift journey. Write daily entries about your progress, challenges you overcome, and moments of realization. This journal will serve as a record of your growth and a source of inspiration in the future.

_____

_____

_____

_____

_____

Lesson 2:
Continuous Testing and Adaptation

Testing Experiment Plan: Select an advertising strategy or platform you're currently using. Design an experiment where you modify one element (e.g., audience targeting, ad copy, visuals) and measure the impact on engagement or conversion rates. Document your hypothesis, changes made, and results observed.

_____

_____

_____

_____

_____

Failure Analysis and Learning: Recall a past advertising campaign that didn't yield the expected results. Write a detailed analysis of what went wrong, what you learned from the failure, and how you can apply those insights to future campaigns. Use this analysis as a guide for continuous improvement.

_____

_____

_____

_____

_____

_____

_____

_____

_____

_____

_____

New Approach Simulation: Imagine you're launching a new advertising campaign from scratch. Write a step-by-step plan that includes the initial testing phase, the criteria for success, and the adaptation strategies you'll implement based on early results. This plan will help you approach new campaigns systematically.

_____

_____

_____

_____

Lesson 3:
Iterative Scaling

Scaling Checklist Development: Create a checklist of key considerations when scaling your advertising efforts. Include aspects like budget allocation, audience expansion, creative optimization, and monitoring performance metrics. This checklist will help you methodically approach scaling your strategies.

_____

_____

_____

_____

_____

_____

_____

_____

_____

_____

Refining Successful Methods: Choose an advertising strategy or approach that has shown promise in generating leads. Write a detailed plan to refine and enhance this method. Consider factors like diversifying creative elements, expanding targeting options, and incorporating feedback from engaged leads.

_____

_____

_____

_____

_____

_____

Affiliate Program Blueprint: Imagine you're launching an affiliate program to scale your lead generation efforts. Outline the steps you'll take to set up the program, recruit affiliates, and provide them with the necessary tools and resources. This blueprint will serve as your guide to implementing an effective affiliate program.

_____

_____

_____

_____

_____

_____

_____

_____

_____

_____

_____

Lesson 4:
Persistence and Refinement

Failure to Success Transformation: Reflect on a specific advertising campaign or strategy that initially failed but later achieved success through persistence and refinement. Write a before-and-after comparison that highlights the changes made, lessons learned, and the impact of your persistence on the campaign's outcomes.

_____

_____

_____

_____

_____

_____

Continuous Improvement Plan: Develop a continuous improvement plan for your lead generation efforts. Outline how you'll review and analyze campaign performance regularly, identify areas for refinement, and implement adjustments based on data-driven insights.

_____

_____

_____

_____

_____

_____

_____

_____

_____

_____

Challenge Reflection Essay: Write an essay reflecting on a significant advertising challenge you faced and overcame. Describe the emotions, obstacles, and strategies you used to navigate the challenge. This essay will serve as a testament to your ability to persevere and refine your approach.

_____

_____

_____

_____

_____

Lesson 5:
Long-Term Perspective

Vision Board Creation: Create a vision board that represents your long-term advertising goals and the journey to achieving a $100M leads machine. Use images, quotes, and visual elements to capture your aspirations and the milestones you'll reach along the way.

_____

_____

_____

_____

_____

_____

_____

_____

_____

_____

_____

Milestone Tracking Journal: Start a journal to track your progress towards building a successful advertising strategy. Document significant milestones, breakthroughs, and lessons learned. This journal will help you maintain a long-term perspective and celebrate your achievements.

_____

_____

_____

_____

_____

_____

_____

_____

Future Success Narrative: Write a narrative describing your business's advertising success three years from now. Detail the strategies, growth rates, and achievements you've reached. This narrative will reinforce your commitment to the long-term journey and inspire you to stay focused on your goals.

_____

_____

_____

_____

_____

_____

_____

_____

_____

_____

_____

Made in United States
Troutdale, OR
03/11/2024

18378431R00090